What Next, Charlie Brown?

Selected Cartoons from
YOU'RE OUT OF YOUR MIND, CHARLIE BROWN!
Vol. II

Charles M. Schulz

CORONET BOOKS
Hodder Fawcett, London

This book comprises the second half of
YOU'RE OUT OF YOUR MIND, CHARLIE BROWN!,
and is published by arrangement with
Holt, Reinhart and Winston, Inc.

Coronet edition 1971
Ninth impression 1979

———————————————————

Printed in Great Britain for Hodder Fawcett Ltd.,
Mill Road, Dunton Green, Sevenoaks, Kent
(Editorial Office: 47 Bedford Square, London WC1 3DP)
by C. Nicholls & Company Ltd
The Philips Park Press, Manchester

ISBN 0 340 12544 6

ALL RIGHT, THEN I'LL LET YOU IN ON THE SECRET..IT'S A LITTLE MUSIC BOX..

HEY, VIOLET! HE GOT YOU A MUSIC BOX!!

AAUGH!

NATURE IS A FASCINATING STUDY, LINUS...

NOW, TAKE THIS TREE. SEE HOW THE BARK IS DAMAGED? IT ALMOST LOOKS LIKE SOMEONE HAS BEEN POUNDING HIS HEAD AGAINST IT...

MOST LIKELY, HOWEVER, IT WAS CAUSED BY A BEAR WHO MERELY STOPPED TO SHARPEN HIS CLAWS!

SIGH WHAT IN THE WORLD WILL SHE BE LIKE WHEN SHE'S A TEEN-AGER?

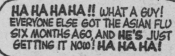

WHAM!

SCHROEDER, I'VE BEEN THINKING...

WHAT IF YOU AND I WERE TO GET MARRIED SOMEDAY, AND HAVE A LOT OF CHILDREN?

AND WHAT IF, INSTEAD OF BEING REAL RICH, WE WERE REAL POOR BECAUSE YOU INSISTED ON PLAYING THE PIANO IN SOME CHEAP LITTLE..

WHAT?

✳ WHEW ✳

EVERY NOW AND THEN I THINK MAYBE I SHOULD MARRY AN ACCORDION PLAYER!

YOU SHOULD'A' SLUGGED HER, CHARLIE BROWN! EVEN IF SHE IS MY SISTER, I SAY YOU SHOULD HAVE SLUGGED HER!

YOU DON'T UNDERSTAND, LINUS... CHARLIE BROWN DID A VERY ADMIRABLE THING.. HE WOULD NEVER THINK OF HITTING A GIRL, SO HE DELIBERATELY HUMILIATED HIMSELF TO HOLD ON TO HIS HIGH MORAL STANDARDS!

ISN'T THAT RIGHT, CHARLIE BROWN?

NO, I WAS JUST AFRAID OF GETTING BEAT UP!

ZOOM!

CLOMP!

AAUGH!

GOOD GRIEF!

CLOMP!

NOBODY!

MAY I HELP YOU WITH YOUR PUZZLE, LUCY?

NO! BESIDES, I'M ALMOST DONE..

PLEASE?

OH, GOOD GRIEF! ALL RIGHT! HERE...YOU CAN PUT IN THE LAST PIECE..

GOOD! NOW, LET ME SEE.. HOW DOES IT GO? DOES IT FIT LIKE THIS, OR DOES IT FIT LIKE THIS? OR MAYBE DOES IT FIT THIS WAY? LET'S SEE NOW...

DOES IT FIT THIS WAY OR THIS WAY OR THIS WAY? OR MAYBE DOES IT FIT THAT WAY?

MAYBE IT FITS LIKE THIS OR AROUND THIS WAY OR MAYBE IT FITS THIS WAY OR LIKE THIS OR MAYBE..

GIMME THAT PIECE!!

SHE NEVER LETS ME HELP WITH ANYTHING..

CHARGE!

HEY! WHAT'RE Y'DOING THERE?!!
WHAT'RE Y'DOING WITH THOSE PLIERS?
HEY!

SCHULZ

CLOMP!

YOU DRIVE
ME CRAZY!

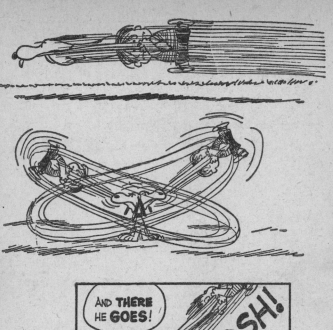

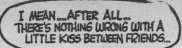

BOY, HOW THAT GIRL CAN DANCE! SHE'S REALLY A BALL OF FIRE! YES, SIR! SHE'S QUITE A GIRL!!

TOO. BAD SHE ISN'T A DOG..

CLOMP! AAUGH!

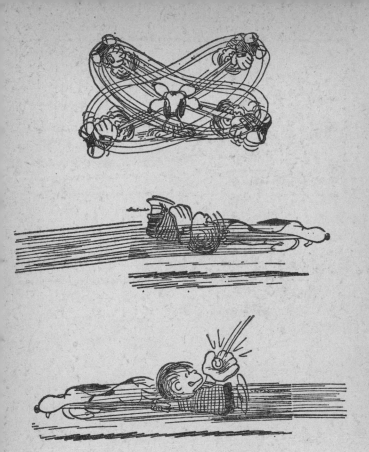

NO MANAGER IN THE HISTORY OF BASEBALL HAS EVER HAD TO GO THROUGH WHAT I HAVE TO GO THROUGH!

© 1970 United Feature Syndicate, Inc.

Wherever Paperbacks Are Sold

ALL THIS AND SNOOPY, TOO

All these books are available at your local bookshop or newsagent, or can be ordered direct from the publisher. Just tick the titles you want and fill in the form below.
Prices and availability subject to change without notice.

CORONET BOOKS, P.O. Box 11, Falmouth, Cornwall.

Please send cheque or postal order, and allow the following for postage and packing:

U.K. – One book 22p plus 10p per copy for each additional book ordered, up to a maximum of 82p.

B.F.P.O. and EIRE – 22p for the first book plus 10p per copy for the next 6 books, thereafter 4p per book.

OTHER OVERSEAS CUSTOMERS – 30p for the first book and 10p per copy for each additional book.

Name ....

Address ....

....